Contents

A swirling storm   4

Ocean storms   6

Hurricane science   14

Hurricane measurements   22

A hurricane is coming   26

A hurricane arrives   32

Going inland   36

Fighting hurricanes   40

Find out more   44

Glossary   46

Index   48

Any words appearing in the text in bold, **like this**, are explained in the Glossary. You can also look out for them in the Stormy words box at the bottom of each page.

A swirling storm

It is late summer in the Caribbean. Usually the sea is quite calm here, but not today. Monster waves are crashing on to the shore. There must be powerful winds out at sea. Soon the sky fills with threatening clouds. The wind starts to blow and heavy rain begins to fall. A hurricane is on the way!

Winds and waves

The winds grow stronger and stronger. It is hard to walk outside. Bands of **torrential** rain lash down. The winds tear things apart. **Debris** from damaged houses, fences and road signs flies about. The sea level rises quickly. Huge waves **surge** over the coast. They smash down houses, wash away cars and buses, and carry boats **inland**. It is chaos everywhere. The terrifying weather lasts for many hours.

The hurricane slowly moves away. A few hours later the sky is blue and the sea is calm again. Behind it is a trail of flooding and destruction.

Hurricane Bonnie arrives at Wilmington Beach, North Carolina in 1998. ▷

cyclone   name given to a hurricane in the southern hemisphere
debris   bits and pieces of wrecked houses, cars and other objects

Turbulent Planet

Violent Skies

Hurricanes

Chris Oxlade

www.raintreepublishers.co.uk
Visit our website to find out more information about **Raintree** books.

To order:
 Phone 44 (0) 1865 888113
Send a fax to 44 (0) 1865 314091
 Visit the Raintree Bookshop at **www.raintreepublishers.co.uk** to browse our catalogue and order online.

First published in Great Britain by Raintree, Halley Court, Jordan Hill, Oxford OX2 8EJ, part of Harcourt Education. Raintree is a registered trademark of Harcourt Education Ltd.

Produced for Raintree Publishers by Discovery Books Ltd.

Editorial: Saskia Besier, Melanie Copland and Carol Usher
Design: Michelle Lisseter and Rob Norridge
Picture Research: Rachel Tisdale
Consultant: Keith Lye
Production: Duncan Gilbert
Printed and bound in China by South China Printing Company
Originated by Ambassador Litho Ltd

ISBN 1 844 43622 5 (hardback)
08 07 06 05 04
10 9 8 7 6 5 4 3 2 1

ISBN 1 844 43628 4 (paperback)
09 08 07 06 05
10 9 8 7 6 5 4 3 2 1

British Library Cataloguing in Publication Data
Oxlade, Chris
Violent skies: hurricanes – (Turbulent planet)
1. Hurricanes – Juvenile literature 2. Natural disasters – Juvenile literature
551.5'52

A full catalogue record for this book is available from the British Library.

Photo acknowledgements

p.4/5, Frank Lane Picture Agency; p.5 top, Science Photo Library/NASA/Goddard Space Flight Center; p.5 middle, Corbis/Annie Griffiths Belt; p.5 bottom, Corbis/Jim McDonald; p.7, Science Photo Library/Carl Purcell; p.7 right, Science Photo Library/James Stevenson; p.8, Science Photo Library/Fritz Henle; p.9, Science Photo Library/ NOAA; p.10/11, Corbis/Stocktrek; p.11, Corbis/Roger Ball; p.12, Panos Pictures/Trygve Bolstad; p.13, Panos Pictures/ Fred Hoogervorst; p.14/15, Frank Lane Picture Agency/ Colin Marshall; p.14, Frank Lane Picture Agency; p.16, Corbis/ Lester Lefkowitz; p.17, Corbis/NASA; p.18, Corbis; p.18 left, Science Photo Library/Chris Saltlberger; p.19, Corbis; p.20, Science Photo Library/2002 Orbital Imaging Corporation; p.21, Science Photo Library/NASA; p.21 right, Corbis/NASA; p.22, Corbis Sygma; p.23, Science Photo Library/Chris Saltlberger; p.24/25, Guy Motil/Corbis; p.24, Corbis/Bettmann; p.25, Corbis/Steve Starr; p.26/27, Corbis/ Galen Rowell; p.27, Frank Lane Picture Agency; p.28, Corbis/Jim McDonald; p.29, Corbis/Post and Courier; p.29 right, Corbis/Alan Schein; p.30/31, Corbis Sygma; p.30, Corbis/Annie Griffiths Belt; p.31, Corbis; p.32, Corbis Sygma; p.33, Corbis/Will & Deni McIntyre; p.34, Corbis/ Steve Starr; p.34 left, Corbis; p.35 Corbis Sygma; p.36/37, Corbis Sygma/Tramontina Gary; p.37, Corbis/Roger Ressmeyer; p.38, Science Photo Library/NASA/Goddard Space Flight Center; p.38 left, Corbis/John Van Hasselt; p.39, Corbis/Yan Arthus-Bertrand; p.40/41, Corbis Sygma; p.40, Corbis; p.41, Science Photo Library/Detlev Ravensway; p.42, Corbis/Kristin Royalty; p.43, Corbis; p.44, Corbis Sygma; p.45, Corbis/Stocktrek.

Cover photograph reproduced with permission of Associated Press

Every effort has been made to contact copyright holders of any material reproduced in this book. Any omissions will be rectified in subsequent printings if notice is given to the publishers.

Disclaimer

Find out later...

What does a hurricane look like?

What is a **storm surge**?

What can you do if a hurricane is coming?

Destructive hurricanes

The strongest winds on Earth belong to **tornadoes**, but hurricanes cause more damage and affect more people. A hurricane can grow to hundreds of miles across. Near the centre its winds blow at more than 240 kilometres (150 miles) per hour. The winds destroy things in the hurricane's path and push up huge waves. These cause terrible floods.

surge sudden rush
tornado spinning column of air that makes contact with the ground

Ocean storms

A hurricane is a huge, swirling storm. Inside are very strong winds and rains. **Meteorologists** call these storms tropical storms. A tropical storm becomes a hurricane when the winds inside it blow faster than 118 kilometres (73 miles) per hour.

Hurricane hot spots

Luckily, you will probably never be in a hurricane. This is because hurricanes only happen in a few parts of the world. They form over very warm seas and oceans in the **tropics**. That is why they are called tropical storms. Hurricanes move away from the **equator**, until they hit colder water or land. Then they die away.

Hurricane words

The word hurricane comes from the word Hurican. This was the name of a local Caribbean storm god. The word typhoon comes from the Cantonese word *tai-fung*, meaning great wind.

This map shows the areas which are most often hit by hurricanes and the places mentioned in this book.

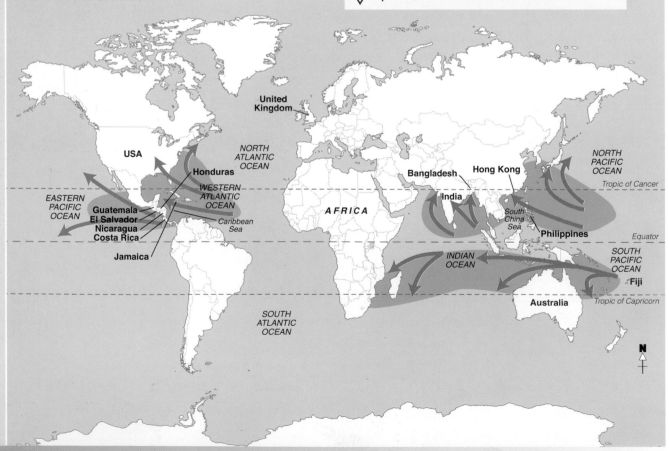

Stormy words equator imaginary line around the Earth, half-way between the poles
eye area in the centre of a hurricane where the winds are calm

More names

Strong tropical storms develop in the Atlantic and the Caribbean Sea. Here they are called hurricanes. In the western North Pacific and China Sea, they are called **typhoons**. Strong tropical storms appear in the Indian Ocean and Australia too. These are called tropical **cyclones**. In this book we normally use the word hurricane. Everything we say about hurricanes is true for typhoons and tropical cyclones too.

Fifteen million trees were blown down during Britain's Great Storm in 1987. ▽

The Great Storm

The Great Storm hit southern Britain in 1987. Although there were winds as strong as a hurricane, it was not a hurricane. A hurricane has an **eye** but this weather system did not.

◁ Waves and high winds from Hurricane Gilbert batter Jamaica in 1988.

meteorologist   scientist who studies and reports on the weather
tropics   area of the world, near the equator, where the weather is warm

Hurricane seasons

Hurricanes only form at certain times of the year. These times are called hurricane **seasons**. In the northern **hemisphere** the hurricane season lasts from June to November. These are the summer and autumn months. By June the sea has warmed up enough for hurricanes to form. After November the sea has cooled down again. A hurricane is most likely to strike in August and September. In the southern hemisphere it is summer and autumn between November and May. This is the hurricane season there.

Never used again

If a hurricane is very damaging, like Hurricane Hugo, its name is never used again. The name is retired and replaced by a new one.

The name Hugo was given to the hurricane that caused this damage. It went on to be the strongest hurricane of 1989. ▷

hemisphere   one half of the Earth
season   time of the year with typical weather

Hurricane names

Meteorologists give each new hurricane, typhoon or tropical cyclone a name. The names identify the different hurricanes. Simple names are easier for people to remember in hurricane warnings. Meteorologists start a new list of names at the beginning of each year. This is in alphabetical order. The first hurricane of the year gets the first name on the list, the second one the second name and so on. There are separate lists for each hurricane region. The list for hurricanes in the Atlantic is made up of boys and girls names. The list for the North Pacific is made up of names of animals and plants. About ten names are used up in the Atlantic region each year.

Pick a name

This is the 2005 hurricane name list for the Atlantic:

Arlene, Bret, Cindy, Dennis, Emily, Franklin, Gert, Harvey, Irene, Jose, Katrina, Lenny, Maria, Nate, Ophelia, Philippe, Rita, Stan, Tammy, Vince, Wilma.

This is a rare sighting of two hurricanes in the Pacific in 1974. Hurricane Ione is at the top and Hurricane Kirsten is at the bottom. ◁

typhoon   name given to a hurricane in the western North Pacific

Hurricane Andrew

A **tropical** storm began over the Atlantic Ocean on 17 August 1992. Hurricane **forecasters** named it Andrew. Hurricane Andrew moved slowly westwards. By 22 August the storm was about 800 kilometres (500 miles) from the coast of the USA. It was a severe storm, but not a hurricane. People were not too worried. The next day, Andrew became more powerful and changed direction. It battered the Bahamas. Then it got even stronger. With winds blowing at more than 240 kilometres (150 miles) per hour it headed straight for Florida.

◁ This is a map showing the path of Hurricane Andrew.

Hurricane Andrew damage

- 61 lives lost
- 20,000 homes destroyed
- 60,000 homes badly damaged
- 200,000 people made homeless
- US $25 billion of damage

These **satellite** images of Hurricane Andrew show how it developed as it moved westwards across the Atlantic. ▷

broadcast send information over the radio or television
forecaster person who gives information about the weather

Andrew makes landfall

Hurricane warnings were **broadcast** for the southern tip of Florida. More than a million people abandoned their homes and drove north to safety. Hurricane Andrew reached land in the early morning of 24 August. The **eye** of the storm hit the southern **suburbs** of the city of Miami.

The sea level rose by 5 metres. Huge waves flooded **inland**. They wrecked homes and shops. The waves picked up boats and dumped them in the streets. Gusts of wind were measured at more than 320 kilometres (200 miles) per hour. The wind ripped thousands of mobile homes to pieces. Vehicles were flipped over like toys. Millions of trees were flattened.

The hurricane went into the Gulf of Mexico. It damaged oil rigs at sea. Then it hit the coast of Louisiana, causing more damage.

Then I drove towards Homestead. I was only halfway there when I began seeing the totally **unbelievable destruction.**

An insurance inspector visiting Homestead, a town south of Miami

△ These are the remains of mobile homes in a park. They were in the path of Hurricane Andrew.

Bangladesh cyclones

When **cyclones** hit the country of Bangladesh, it suffers badly. Most of Bangladesh is made up of a huge **delta**. This is a low-lying area where many rivers flow into the sea. Millions of poor farmers live and work on Bangladesh's deltas.

Cyclones often move through the Bay of Bengal and land in Bangladesh. Waves **surge** across the delta and cause terrible flooding. Poor **communications** make it difficult to warn people. Bad roads delay their escape.

Dangerous floods

People often talk about the strong winds of hurricanes. But flooding along the coast causes the most deaths. The cyclones in Bangladesh show this.

Flooding in the streets of Dhaka, △ the capital of Bangladesh, in 1998.

communication   way of giving and receiving information
delta   wide fan-shaped piece of land, where a river empties into the sea

Cyclone 2B

The giant storm known as Cyclone 2B hit Bangladesh on 29 April 1991. Its winds blew at a speed of 235 kilometres (145 miles) per hour. A wall of sea water, 6 metres high, surged across the low-lying coast. Warnings were given on national radio. Thousands of people squeezed into hurricane shelters, but millions were left outside. The winds and waves destroyed more than a million homes. Tens of thousands of people were drowned. They could not escape to higher ground. Altogether 140,000 people died. Since this disaster, more hurricane shelters have been built in Bangladesh.

△ These women are tending rice paddies in Bangladesh.

The damage caused by cyclones in Bangladesh is so great because it is a very poor country. It also has a large population. Warning systems are not as advanced as in wealthier parts of the world.

Hurricane facts

A cyclone hit Bangladesh in 1970. Giant waves swept across the delta. They destroyed millions of rice **paddies**. Millions of cattle were drowned too. About 300,000 people died. This was one of the worst natural disasters ever to happen in the world.

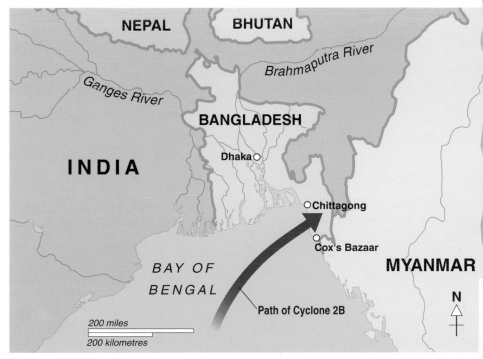

◁ This is a map of Bangladesh. Cyclones sweep in from the Bay of Bengal.

paddy   water-filled field used for growing rice

Hurricane science

Hurricanes bring damaging, violent winds and heavy rain, but they start their lives in warm places. They begin over tropical seas and oceans. Sunshine is always very strong in the **tropics**. The strong sunshine heats the surfaces of seas and oceans. The water gets very warm. This means it contains heat energy. Hurricanes need this energy to form and keep going.

Hurricane from above

A hurricane is an enormous storm. From above a hurricane looks like a great, white swirl with the dark ocean underneath. Around the edges are ragged, spiralling arms of cloud. Right in the middle is an area called the **eye**. Inside the eye the winds are calm.

Small and deadly

Bad does not always mean big! **Cyclone** Tracy was very **compact**. At 48 kilometres from the eye the winds were light, but the centre of the storm destroyed Darwin, Australia.

This shows the devastation in Darwin created when Cyclone Tracy swept ◁ through the town in 1974.

compact   closely packed together
cumulonimbus   enormous thunder clouds up to 10 kilometres high

Hurricane structure

Great towering thunderclouds make up a hurricane. These can be thousands of metres high. They are called **cumulonimbus** clouds. The storm clouds form into round bands, with spaces between them. There may be hundreds of severe thunderstorms inside a hurricane. Lightning flashes through the clouds and **torrential** rain pours out of them.

This is what the inside of a hurricane looks like. The arrow shows the direction ▽ it is spinning.

surface of the sea

Hurricane sizes

A typical hurricane is about 480 kilometres (300 miles) across. Some are as big as 960 kilometres (600 miles) across. They are more than 8 kilometres (5 miles) high.

△ This is Fiji in the Pacific Ocean. The tropical storms that turn into hurricanes form over warm seas like this.

water vapour   water in the form of a gas

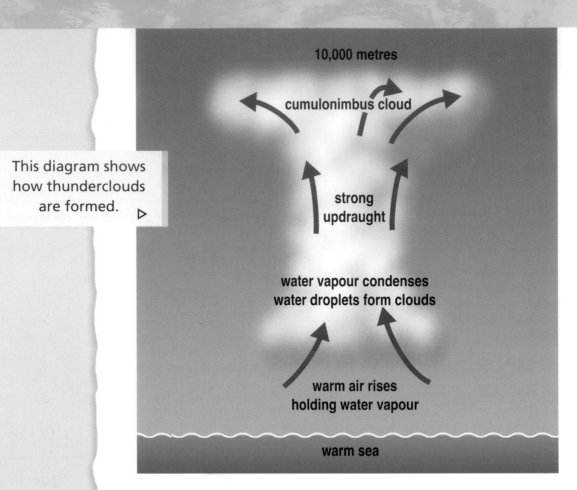

10,000 metres

cumulonimbus cloud

strong updraught

water vapour condenses
water droplets form clouds

warm air rises
holding water vapour

warm sea

This diagram shows how thunderclouds are formed. ▷

Hurricane formation

The water temperature must be at least 27 °C before a hurricane can form. The warm seawater heats the air above its surface. The warm air is good at holding **water vapour**. A lot of water **evaporates** from the water surface into the air. The warm air is very moist.

Storm energy

Hurricanes have lots of energy. Scientists have worked out how much energy a hurricane makes in one day. It is enough electricity to last the whole of the USA for six months.

The incredible energy in a hurricane would run the millions of lights of Las Vegas ◁ for many years.

condense   turn from gas into liquid
evaporate   turn from liquid to gas

Forming clouds

Warm air always rises upwards, if there is cooler air around and above it. You can see this effect when hot smoky air rises from a bonfire. The warm, moist air over the warm ocean rises and slowly cools. The water vapour **condenses** to form tiny water droplets. The same thing happens when you breathe on a cold mirror. The water droplets collect together and form clouds over the ocean.

Towering storms

When the water vapour condenses it gives out heat. This heat keeps the air warm and the air continues to rise. The rising air forms strong **updraughts**. The updraughts only stop when they reach to about 10,000 metres above the surface. Incredibly high **cumulonimbus** clouds are formed.

Hurricane seedlings

A **seedling** is a group of thunderstorms. These may turn into a hurricane. About a hundred seedlings form over the Atlantic each year. Only about one in ten of them becomes a **tropical** storm. About half of these tropical storms become hurricanes, **typhoons** or **cyclones**.

A group of thunderstorms over an ocean, seen from a **satellite** high in space.

seedling group of thunderstorms that may turn into a hurricane
updraught rising air

The eye of the storm

There is always a calm area right in the centre of a hurricane. It is called the **eye**. The eye is very small compared to the hurricane. Normally it is between 8 and 24 kilometres (5 and 15 miles) across. Some eyes are as small as 5 kilometres (3 miles) across and some are as large as 64 kilometres (40 miles) across. The eye is a strange place. If you travel towards the middle of a hurricane the winds get faster and faster, but in the eye the wind is calm. The air is also clear. From above you can see straight through the hurricane to the ocean below. On the water's surface are chaotic, giant waves. They are caused by the violent winds around the eye.

△ This is inside the eye of Hurricane Floyd. It was photographed in 1999 from the aircraft of a hurricane-hunting team.

△ The eye of Hurricane Isabel was photographed from the International Space Station in September 2003.

The eye wall

Inside the eye, it is like being inside a giant tin can. Circular walls of cloud up to 10 kilometres high surround you. This wall of cloud is called the **eye wall**. It is made up of towering thunderclouds. The hurricane's most violent winds are in the clouds of the eye wall. The smaller the eye, the stronger the winds are. The severe thunderstorms in the eye wall often cause **tornadoes** to form. Tornadoes have winds even stronger than hurricanes. Sometimes seabirds fly about in the eye. They are trapped there because they cannot fly through the violent winds in the eye wall.

Hurricane Camille

The smaller the eye, the more violent the winds around it. Hurricane Camille hit Mississippi in 1969. Up to that year it was the most destructive hurricane to hit the USA. Its eye was just 7 kilometres (4 miles) across.

This damage was caused by Hurricane Camille's winds. They reached more than ▽ 320 kilometres (200 miles) per hour.

Spinning storms

A **seedling** thunderstorm cannot turn into a hurricane straight away. It must become a **tropical** storm first. A tropical storm is a huge spinning storm, but its winds are weaker than the winds of a hurricane. Only a few seedlings turn into a tropical storm. Most just die away. This happens because of the way the Earth **rotates**.

If a seedling storm forms close to the **equator** it quickly dies away. But at **latitudes** more than 5° away from the equator the storm seedling begins to spin slowly. It moves slowly westwards. This is because the Earth is rotating.

A storm near Australia, in the southern hemisphere, spins clockwise. ▽

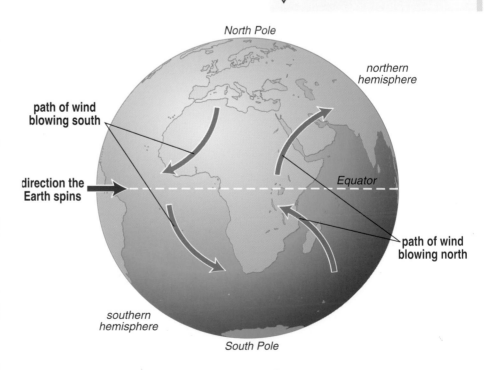

This diagram shows the curved path of winds over the Earth's surface. ▽

North Pole

northern hemisphere

path of wind blowing south

direction the Earth spins

Equator

path of wind blowing north

southern hemisphere

South Pole

The Coriolis effect

Think about a wind blowing to the north, towards the North Pole. Instead of blowing in a straight line, it follows a curved path over the Earth's surface. This is because of the spin of the Earth and the atmosphere. This is called the Coriolis effect. It explains why storms begin to rotate.

anticlockwise   moving in the opposite direction to the hands of a clock
clockwise   direction that the hands of a clock move round

Storm to hurricane

Warm, moist air goes into the storm. Its energy makes the storm spin faster. The storm's winds increase. If the winds reach 62 kilometres (39 miles) per hour or more, the storm is known as a tropical storm. The storm keeps growing as long as there is warm, moist air to feed it. If it moves farther from the equator it spins faster and faster. When its winds reach 118 kilometres (73 miles) per hour then it is officially a hurricane. Only about half of all tropical storms become hurricanes. Tropical storms always rotate **anticlockwise** if they develop in the northern **hemisphere**. In the southern hemisphere they always rotate **clockwise**.

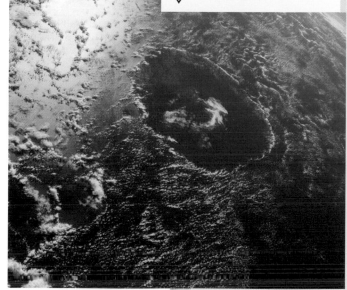

This thunderstorm is dying away.
▽

This photograph of Hurricane Fran over the Caribbean Sea, in the northern hemisphere, shows it is spinning anticlockwise. ▽

Dying storms

Most tropical storms and hurricanes die out before they hit land. Some move over cool seas and they lose their supply of energy. Others move close to the equator, where there is nothing to keep them spinning.

latitude   distance north or south of the equator, measured in degrees
rotate   turn round or twist

Hurricane measurements

Meteorologists measure the speed and direction of wind, rainfall, **air pressure** and temperature. But how do they measure hurricanes? The answer is by their strength or **intensity**. The intensity measures how strong the winds are and how much damage the hurricane does when it reaches land.

Rare hurricanes

Very severe hurricanes are rare. Only four category 5 hurricanes hit the USA in the whole of the twentieth century.

The category 4 Hurricane Luis battered Guadeloupe in the Caribbean in 1995.

air pressure   force of air pressing down on the Earth
category   group or class of things

The Saffir-Simpson Scale

The **international** scale for measuring hurricanes is the Saffir-Simpson hurricane scale. There are five **categories** of hurricane in this scale. Category 1 is the weakest or least intense. Category 5 is the strongest or most intense. The wind speeds in the list are **sustained** wind speeds. This means the winds blow at this speed most of the time during the worst part of the storm.

Saffir and Simpson

Herbert Saffir was an engineer and Robert Simpson was a meteorologist. They developed the Saffir-Simpson hurricane scale. They worked at the National Hurricane Center in Florida, USA.

Staff at the National Hurricane Center in the USA watch the progress of Hurricane Floyd. This hurricane reached category 4 strength. ▷

The Saffir-Simpson Scale

Category	Wind speed	Damage
1	118–152 kilometres (73–94 miles) per hour	Not much damage to buildings. Some trees fall. Mobile homes move. Some flooding on coasts.
2	153–176 kilometres (95–109 miles) per hour	Roofs, doors and windows broken. Many trees fall. Piers damaged. Small boats swept ashore. Flooding of low-lying coasts.
3	177–208 kilometres (110–129 miles) per hour	Structures of buildings damaged. Mobile homes destroyed. Flooding up to 10 kilometres **inland**.
4	209–248 kilometres (130–154 miles) per hour	Some roofs torn off and walls collapse. Beaches **eroded** away. Large boats swept inland. Severe flooding up to 10 kilometres inland.
5	more than 248 kilometres (154 miles) per hour	Some buildings destroyed by wind. Buildings near coast swept away by waves. Severe flooding up to 16 kilometres inland.

erosion   wearing away by action of water or wind
sustain   keep at a certain strength or level all the time

Hurricane winds

Hurricanes are famous for their winds. A **category** 5 hurricane has **sustained** wind speeds of more than 248 kilometres (154 miles) per hour around its **eye**. Gusts of winds can reach 320 kilometres (200 miles) per hour. There are mini **tornadoes** in the **eye wall**. These have even stronger winds. When the strong winds blow across many kilometres of ocean they whip up huge waves. In the Pacific the waves can be 25 metres high. This is the same height as a six-storey building. These waves can swamp even the biggest ships.

Fifi floods

Hurricane Fifi hit Central America in 1974. Torrential rain fell on Honduras, El Salvador, Guatemala and Belize. Sixty-three centimetres of rain fell in a day. Floods and landslides killed 8000 people.

◁ Houses in Honduras surrounded by muddy flood waters after Hurricane Fifi passed by.

A hurricane's winds create dangerous seas. ▷

flash flood   quickly developing flood

Six-metre waves crash against the shore on Palm Beach, Florida. ▷

Surge heights

A hurricane storm surge can easily reach 5 metres high. The highest storm surge we know about measured about 13 metres. It hit Australia in 1899.

The storm surge

The **air pressure** in the centre of a hurricane is lower than the air pressure outside the hurricane. This is because the air is rising in the centre. This low pressure allows the water underneath the hurricane to push upwards. This makes a wide bulge in the sea's surface. The bulge is made higher by the wind. The wind pushes the bulge forwards ahead of the storm. When a hurricane hits a coast the water washes right over low-lying land. This rush of water is called a **storm surge**. It is the most dangerous feature of a hurricane.

Rain storms

A big hurricane can pick up 2 billion tonnes of water a day through **evaporation** from the sea. This water falls back to the Earth as **torrential** rain. A hurricane can drop a year's worth of rain in a few hours. If this happens over land, the rain causes **flash floods**.

Moving a city

In 1961 Hurricane Hattie caused a storm surge. This destroyed 75 per cent of the buildings in Belize City. This is the capital of Belize in Central America. Two hundred people died. A new capital city, called Belmopan, was built 80 kilometres (50 miles) **inland**. There it is safe from future hurricanes.

storm surge   sudden rise in sea level that happens as a hurricane approaches land

A hurricane is coming

What is it like to be in the path of a **category** 4 hurricane? What would you do to protect yourself from this monster storm? What happens to towns and cities when a hurricane thunders through? How do places recover afterwards? Let us see what happens when a hurricane forms and hits the southern coast of the USA.

Storms at sea

A group of thunderstorms forms over the warm, **tropical** ocean, near the west coast of Africa. It is a hurricane **seedling**. It is over 1600 kilometres (1000 miles) from the USA and it will take over a week to arrive there. However, images from weather **satellites** show it exists. The seedling is being watched!

Map to show the path △ of our category 4 hurricane.

Gaining strength

Gradually the seedling begins to spin. It turns from several groups of storms into one large spinning storm. A few days later, it has grown into a tropical storm. Hurricane **forecasters** monitor it closely on their satellite images. It is moving westwards at 24 kilometres (15 miles) per hour. Each day it spins faster, as it takes energy from the warm sea. Finally a small area appears in the storm's centre. It is an **eye**. A new hurricane has formed!

Hurricane forecasters send aircraft out to measure conditions inside the hurricane. **Data** from the aircraft shows that winds near the eye are blowing at more than 160 kilometres (100 miles) per hour. Ships sail north or south to avoid the approaching storm.

This group of thunderstorm clouds could be the start of a new hurricane. ▽

△ The deck of an American aircraft carrier damaged by a typhoon in the Pacific Ocean in 1945.

The hurricane continues on its path towards the USA. About 36 hours before a hurricane is likely to hit land, **forecasters broadcast** a hurricane watch on television and radio. Most people know exactly what to do. They begin their family disaster plans.

Disaster supply kit

People in hurricane hot spots keep a supply kit handy. It might contain:

- canned foods
- camping stove
- pans
- blankets
- wet-weather clothes
- first-aid kit
- torch and spare batteries
- radio and spare batteries
- money
- tools
- drinking water.

Disaster plan

- Fix strong wooden shutters over the windows
- Lock away loose objects such as garden chairs
- Check the contents of disaster supply kits (see left)
- Store plenty of fresh water in containers
- Buy enough food to last for a few days

These workers are fitting wooden shutters to windows as Hurricane Hugo approached in 1989. ▷

Evacuation

The next morning, the hurricane is still on its way. A hurricane warning is broadcast. This means the hurricane is going to hit in the next 24 hours. People living right in the path of the hurricane are advised to **evacuate** their homes.

There is no time to waste. Most people load their cars with supply kits, water, food and pets. Then they head for the nearest **evacuation route**. Thousands of other people are leaving too. It may take hours to get through the long traffic jams. When they reach safety people try to find hotel rooms, but others just camp in their cars.

The most at risk areas in the USA have special places where people can shelter. These are large, safe buildings, such as schools. The elderly are usually moved there first.

SUBJECT: Hurricane Watch
TIME: 6.00 pm Tuesday 6 May

The Hurricane Prediction Center has issued a hurricane watch for southern Florida. Hurricane Barbara (**category** 4) is predicted to hit land at 6.00 AM Thursday 8 May. **Sustained** winds of 240 kilometres (150 miles) per hour and a **storm surge** of 4 metres are likely. People in low-lying areas are advised to prepare to **evacuate**.

Follow the signs

In many hurricane hot spots the authorities carefully work out the best evacuation routes for people to take. This helps people to escape quickly. The routes are marked with special signs.

Evacuation routes often grind to a halt as thousands of people try to leave cities at the same time. ▽

EVACUATION ROUTE

evacuation route   path followed to get to a safe place

First signs

The hurricane is still hundreds of miles out to sea. Its **eye** will not arrive for many hours yet, but the hurricane is on its way. The wind is picking up. The waves crashing on the shore are getting larger. Gradually the sky clouds over.

Now it begins to rain. The rain lashes down for more than an hour. All the time the wind gets stronger. The waves get bigger and closer together. The **air pressure** is falling quickly. People can tell this by looking at their **barometers**. The eye of the storm is on its way!

Boats are often carried inland by storm surges. Cyclone Luis picked up this boat in 1995. ▽

△ Large waves created by Hurricane Felix crash into beach houses in Virginia, USA in 1995.

barometer   instrument that measures air pressure

Storm surge

Now the sea level rises quickly. The **storm surge** has arrived. Overall, the sea rises 4 metres above its normal level. Soon the water is washing over the coast. It rushes through the empty streets into homes and shops. Everything is under water. Huge waves wash **inland**. They carry cars and bits of houses with them. Boats from the harbour are piled up in a car park. Buildings along the shore are wrecked by the waves. They collapse into the sea. Wooden houses float off their **foundations** and are smashed up.

Snake trouble

Animals are also in danger from a storm surge. Snakes swim through the water, trying to find dry land. They are usually scared. They often bite, if people get near them in the water.

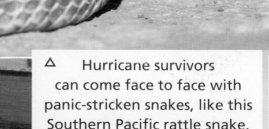

△ Hurricane survivors can come face to face with panic-stricken snakes, like this Southern Pacific rattle snake.

foundation   heavy base that a building stands on

A hurricane arrives

Howling winds

The **eye** of the hurricane is just a few miles away. The **eye wall** is right overhead. This is the most violent part of the storm. The wind is screaming. Some gusts are over 320 kilometres (200 miles) per hour. Rain is lashing down. Flashes of lightning streak across the dark sky.

The wind creates **havoc**. Trees tumble to the ground with their roots ripped out. The falling trees crush cars and houses. Telegraph poles fall. Traffic lights and lamp-posts sway wildly. Cars roll and trucks flip over. The street is a dangerous place to be. Roof tiles, sheets of metal and plastic, signs, garden furniture and other **debris** fly about. They are like deadly **missiles**.

Measuring the wind

It is often impossible to measure the strongest gusts of wind during a hurricane. Wind measuring instruments, called anemometers, are normally wrecked by winds of more than 250 kilometres (155 miles) per hour.

Hurricane watchers took this photograph of a wrecked petrol station in the middle of a hurricane. ▽ It is a dangerous hobby!

A couple examine the damage to their home in South Carolina, USA, after it was hit by Hurricane Hugo in 1989.

◁

Camille party

In 1969 a group of 25 people decided to stay in their apartments in Mississippi for a hurricane party. When Hurricane Camille hit, the wind and **storm surge** swept the apartment block away. Nobody survived.

The eye passes

Now suddenly the winds die away. The sky clears and the sun shines. The hurricane seems to have gone, but this should not fool you. The light winds and clear sky mean that the hurricane's eye has arrived. There will only be a short rest from the howling wind. After only half an hour the wind starts again. The eye has passed by. Now the wind blows from the south-west.

Small houses are ripped apart by the wind. Others lose their roofs. The winds tear through a town centre. They pull windows from office blocks. Glass crashes into the streets below.

missile rocket used as a weapon

The hurricane ends

It is twelve hours since the hurricane's **eye** passed. The wind has died down. The sea is calm. There was more heavy rain, but now it has stopped. The sky is blue and the sun is shining. There is still seawater in the street. This poured **inland** on the **storm surge**. It is draining slowly back into the ocean.

Rebuilding Galveston

In 1900 Galveston, Texas, was destroyed by a hurricane. Galveston now has a 5–metre barrier along the coast to stop storm surges coming inland.

△ The shattered remains of wooden houses in Galveston in 1900.

△ Mobile home parks are often completely wrecked by hurricane-force winds. This damage was caused by Hurricane Andrew in 1992.

aid agency   group which helps people in need, usually in developing countries
bacteria   living things that can only be seen under a microscope

People who **evacuated** are returning home. They find devastation all around. The hurricane has completely destroyed some parts of the town. People who lived here have lost their homes. Their possessions have been ruined by seawater. The streets are full of mud and sand. Vehicles and boats lie in tangled heaps.

Cleaning up

The hurricane caused all that damage in just a few hours, but it will take many months to clear up the mess. The emergency services begin to search for missing people. People without homes go to emergency shelters. The hurricane has damaged electricity supplies, telephone lines and water pipes. These services are repaired as soon as possible. **Debris** is cleared from the streets. Builders begin repairing and rebuilding houses and other buildings.

Hurricane damage is often worse in **developing countries**. People have very little even before a hurricane hits. They may have nothing at all afterwards. **Aid agencies** often help to rescue people. They provide food and clean water. They repair **communications** and homes.

Disease spreads

Disease is often a problem after a hurricane. **Sewage** from flooded drains and **bacteria** from rotting dead animals makes water dangerous to drink. Diseases can spread quickly.

Emergency water supplies waiting to be handed out after Hurricane Andrew.

developing country   poor country that is trying to improve its living conditions
sewage   mixture of waste from toilets and drains

Going inland

Useful rain

Hurricane rainfall is often an important source of water in some dry areas. About a quarter of all rainfall comes from hurricanes and **typhoons** in south-east USA, in parts of South-East Asia and Japan. Hurricanes do one good thing, at least!

For people on the coast the worst is over, but the hurricane does not stop there. It carries on going **inland**. Remember that a hurricane gets its energy from the warm ocean water. When a hurricane moves over land it cannot get any more energy. It begins to die down, but very slowly. It may last for many more days and do a lot more damage.

Wind and rain

Although the hurricane's winds lose strength, they still blow strongly enough to damage trees and buildings inland. However **torrential** rain begins to fall, and it keeps falling for hours on end.

Hurricane facts

A hurricane can dump lots of water over land. Big hurricanes have been known to drop 125 centimetres of rain in a single day. Some places receive that much rain, or less, in a whole year.

Flash floods

Streams and rivers fill up very quickly because so much rain falls. They overflow their banks and flood the landscape. These are **flash floods**. They happen so quickly that people have no time to escape. Roads, bridges, farms and buildings are washed away. The rain mixes with earth to make mud. The mud slides down river valleys. It flows into buildings and sets solid.

Now the storm's winds have slowed right down. It is no longer a hurricane, but a **tropical** storm. The storm moves north across the USA and then out to sea. It loses more energy and finally dies away.

Flash floods caused by hurricanes often catch people without warning. The owners of these cars have left them.
▽

Pinatubo mudslides

Typhoon Yuna crossed the Philippines in 1991. A volcano called Mount Pinatubo erupted at exactly the same time. The typhoon's rains mixed with ash from the eruption. This made a heavy **slurry**. It pushed in roofs and formed deadly **mudslides**. These killed hundreds of people.

△ This is the sort of damage that a mudslide can do. This disaster happened in the Philippines in February 1992.

slurry   half-liquid mixture like mud or cement

> "We don't have anything to eat and no way of making money to buy food."
>
> Teenage victim, Honduras, after Hurricane Mitch

Hurricane Mitch

Hurricane Mitch was a **category** 5 hurricane. It hit Central America in October 1998. Although the winds blew at more than 240 kilometres (150 miles) per hour, the rain from Hurricane Mitch did the most damage. Mitch moved slowly through the Caribbean. Then it slowed almost to a stop over Honduras. In one day it dropped 63 centimetres of rain on Honduras and its neighbouring countries. These are all poor countries. Most people are farmers. They live in simple homes and grow crops.

31 October 1998

Slide of death

Hurricane Mitch's **torrential** rains have triggered disaster in north-west Nicaragua. Inches of rain mixed with volcanic ash from the Casitas volcano formed a deadly **slurry**. This hurtled down the mountainside. Thousands of people are buried.

△ These survivors are wearing masks because of fumes from dead bodies. They escaped a mudslide in Nicaragua, caused by Hurricane Mitch.

△ This **satellite** image taken on 26 October 1998 shows Hurricane Mitch just off the coast of Honduras.

economy   way a country makes money for its people
exports   goods sent out for sale in another country

Floods and mudslides

The rains caused terrible floods. Rivers grew into raging **torrents**. They swept away houses, people and animals. Some people were carried right out to sea. Hillsides became soaked. Eventually they collapsed. This created powerful **mudslides** full of rock. They ripped through towns and killed about 10,000 people.

Mitch's devastation

Hurricane Mitch drifted away, the rain stopped and the floods gradually drained away. They left behind a scene of muddy chaos. Tens of thousands of people had no houses, no fresh water, food or electricity. Roads and bridges were washed away. This made it almost impossible to get food, water and medical supplies to victims. Honduras was helped to recover by aid money, mostly from the USA.

Ruined economies

The **economies** of Honduras, Guatemala and Costa Rica depend on **exports** of bananas, coffee and sugar cane. Hurricane Mitch ruined these crops in 1998. The countries are still trying to recover.

Guanaja in Honduras was devastated by Hurricane Mitch in 1998.

torrent   rushing stream of water

Fighting hurricanes

Dozens of people die in hurricanes every year. Hurricanes also cause millions of dollars of damage. We cannot stop hurricanes, but we can try to **forecast** where and when they will hit land. To forecast hurricanes we need to know how they will behave.

Hurricane forecasting

Pictures from weather **satellites** are very useful. They show the exact position of **seedlings**, **tropical** storms and hurricanes. Hurricane **forecasters** can measure the size of the **eye** from them too. Accurate measurements of wind speeds and **air pressures** are also needed. 'Hurricane Hunter' aircraft fly into storms to collect this information. This **data** is then put into computer programs. These programs can predict where the hurricane will hit land. Then **meteorologists** can **broadcast** warnings.

Before satellites

The first weather satellites were launched into space in the 1960s. Before this, it was almost impossible for forecasters to keep track of hurricanes. So hurricanes often hit without warning.

This weather satellite sends back photographs of the **atmosphere** ◁ every half hour.

Stormy words   computer model   computer program used to predict things
Doppler radar   type of radar that can detect objects and measure speed

Hurricane research

Hurricanes are difficult for forecasters to **predict**. They often change speed direction or strength. Hurricanes often land in places where they are not expected. Researchers try to find out why hurricanes change direction. Here are some ways they do this:

- Study measurements from previous hurricanes
- Find out how water temperatures change when hurricanes pass by
- Try to link the pattern of hurricanes with other world weather patterns, such as the **El Niño** ocean current.

Researchers use this information to make their **computer models** better. There is still a lot for researchers to find out and understand.

Although there are usually some bumps on the way through, they are nothing that the airplane can't handle!

Hurricane Hunter crew member

A giant thunderstorm like this could be the first sign that a new hurricane is about to be born. ▽

Hurricane chasers measure △ wind speeds using a special instrument called a **Doppler radar**.

El Niño pattern of wind and ocean currents that brings extreme weather
forecast give information about something that might happen

41

Be prepared

Your chances of surviving a hurricane are quite high. In fact, nearly all people live to tell the tale. You are not likely to die if you are well prepared. You should plan what to do when a hurricane strikes. You must know where to listen for hurricane warnings. If you practise your escape plan regularly, you will remember what to do when the real thing happens. For example, you could ask your parents to drive along the **evacuation route**.

Safer and safer

More and more people are living in hurricane hot spots. About 15 per cent of the world's population are at risk. But the number of people hurricanes kill and injure is decreasing. This is because of better **forecasting** and warnings.

△   Members of the US Air Force track the progress of Hurricane Isabel in 2003.

Hurricane survival guide

- Check if you live in an **evacuation** area
- Find out what would happen to your home if there were high winds, a **storm surge** or flooding
- Do not forget your pets
- Prepare a survival kit
- At the start of a hurricane season check your supply kit (see page 28) and check your window and door shutters are ready
- During the hurricane season listen to weather forecasts regularly
- If a hurricane is on the way follow the advice given in warnings
- Follow your family's disaster plan
- Evacuate if you are asked to

eye   area in the centre of a hurricane where the winds are calm
forecast   give information about something that might happen

Controlling hurricanes

Many people ask if we can control hurricanes. Would it be possible to weaken a hurricane or make it change course to miss people's homes? Weather experts have had some interesting ideas. One idea is to drop salt or ice into a hurricane. This could make the **eye** grow bigger. The winds become weaker when the eye is bigger. At the moment we don't understand hurricanes well enough to work out how to control them. We could even make things worse.

Hurricane resistant

Are there buildings strong enough to resist hurricanes? The answer is yes. Skyscrapers, stadiums and bridges must all be able to survive hurricane-force winds. But it is too costly to make ordinary houses hurricane proof.

Hong Kong's towering skyscrapers are designed to withstand the winds that could hit during a **typhoon**. ▽

typhoon   name given to a hurricane in the western North Pacific

43

Find out more

Organizations

The Weather Channel

This website run by the USA's television weather channel has a weather encyclopedia, plus news, **forecasts** and historical information about weather.
www.weather.com

BBC Weather

Here you will find forecasts, news and features all about the weather.
www.bbc.co.uk/weather

BBC News

This is a useful site for news about droughts and other extreme weather events.
www.bbc.co.uk

Books

Disasters in Nature: Hurricanes
    Catherine Chambers (Heinemann Library, 2000)
Nature on the Rampage: Hurricanes
    Christy Steele (Raintree, 2004)

World Wide Web

If you want to find out more about hurricanes, you can search the Internet using keywords like these:

- hurricane +news +[date you are interested in]
- Bangladesh +**cyclones**
- wind +**El Niño** +hurricanes

You can also find your own keywords by using headings or words from this book. Use the search tips on page 45 to help you find the most useful websites.

Search tips

There are billions of pages on the Internet, so it can be difficult to find exactly what you are looking for. For example, if you just type in 'wind' on a search engine like Google, you could get a list of millions of web pages. These tips will help you find useful websites more quickly:

- Decide exactly what you want to find out about first
- Use simple keywords instead of whole sentences
- Use two to six keywords in a search, putting the most important words first
- Be precise. Use names of people, places or things when you can.
- If your keywords are made up of two or more words that go together, put quote marks around them, for example "wind damage"
- Use the +sign to join keywords together, for example weather +disaster
- Adding +KS3 to your keywords may help you find web pages at the right level.

Where to search

Search engine

A search engine looks through the entire web. It matches the words in the search box and links them to web sites. They can give thousands of links, but the best matches are at the top of the list, on the first page. Try www.bbc.co.uk

Search directory

A search directory is more like a library of websites. A person has sorted these instead of a computer. You can search by keywords or subject and browse through different sites in the same way you would look through books on a library shelf. A good example is www.yahooligans.com

Glossary

aid agency   group which helps people in need, usually in developing countries

air pressure   force of air pressing down on the Earth

anticlockwise   moving in the opposite direction to the hands of a clock

atmosphere   layer of gases that surround the Earth

bacteria   living things that can only be seen under a microscope

barometer   instrument that measures air pressure

broadcast   send information over the radio or television

category   group or class of things

clockwise   direction that the hands of a clock move round

communication   way of giving and receiving information

compact   closely packed together

computer model   computer program used to predict things

condensation   when a gas turns into a liquid

condense   turn from gas into liquid

cumulonimbus   enormous thunder clouds up to 10 kilometres high

cyclone   name given to a hurricane in the southern hemisphere

data   information, usually in the form of facts or statistics

debris   bits and pieces of wrecked houses, cars and other objects

delta   wide fan-shaped piece of land, where a river empties into the sea

developing country   poor country that is trying to improve its living conditions

Doppler radar   type of radar that can detect objects and measure speed

economy   way a country makes money for its people

El Niño   pattern of wind and ocean currents that brings extreme weather

equator   imaginary line around the Earth, half-way between the poles

erosion   wearing away by action of water or wind

evacuate   leave home and go to a safe place

evacuation route   path followed to get to a safe place

evaporate   turn from liquid to gas

exports   goods sent out for sale in another country

eye   area in the centre of a hurricane where the winds are calm

eye wall   wall of tall clouds around the eye of a hurricane

flash flood   quickly developing flood

forecast   give information about something that might happen

forecaster   person who gives information about the weather

foundation heavy base that a building stands on

havoc great disorder and devastation

hemisphere one half of the Earth

inland away from the coast

intensity strength

international used in or to do with many countries

latitude distance north or south of the equator, measured in degrees

meteorologist scientist who studies and reports on the weather

missile rocket used as a weapon

mudslide mixture of water and earth that slides down a hillside or river

paddy water-filled field used for growing rice

predict say what will happen in the future

rotate turn round or twist

satellite object that observes the Earth from space

season time of the year with typical weather

seedling group of thunderstorms that may turn into a hurricane

sewage mixture of waste from toilets and drains

slurry half-liquid mixture of mud or cement

storm surge sudden rise in sea level that happens as a hurricane approaches land

suburb area of houses on the edge of a city

surge sudden rush

sustain keep at a certain strength or level all the time

tornado spinning column of air that makes contact with the ground

torrent rushing stream of water

torrential great downpour of rain

tropics area of the world, near the equator, where the weather is warm

typhoon name given to a hurricane in the western North Pacific

updraught rising air

water vapour water in the form of a gas

Index

aid 35, 39
air 17–18, 21–2, 25
air pressure 22, 25, 30, 40
aircraft 18, 27, 40
animals 13, 31
Atlantic Ocean 6–7, 9–10, 17–18
Australia 6–7, 14, 21, 25

Bahamas 6, 10
Bangladesh 6, 12–13
Belize 24–5
Belmopan 25
birds 19
Britain 6–7
buildings 43

Caribbean 4, 6, 22, 38
Caribbean Sea 6–7, 21
casualties 13, 27, 37–8, 40
China Sea 6–7
clouds 4, 14–17, 19, 30
communications 12, 35
computers 40–1
Coriolis effect 20
Costa Rica 6, 39
crops 39
Cyclone 2B 13
cyclones 4, 7, 9, 12–14, 17, 30

damage 4–5, 10–11, 22–3,
    35–6, 38–40
Darwin, Australia 14
debris 4, 31–2, 35
developing countries 12–13, 35
disaster plans 28
diseases 35
Doppler radar 41

El Niño 41
El Salvador 42
emergency services 35
energy 14, 16, 21–2, 26–7,
    36–7
equator 6, 20–1
evacuation 29, 35, 42
evacuation routes 29, 35, 42
eyes of hurricanes 7, 11, 14,
    18–19, 24, 27, 30, 32–4,
    40, 43
eye walls 19, 24, 32

Fiji 6, 15
floods 4–5, 11–13, 24–5, 31,
    37, 39, 42
Florida 6, 10–11, 23
forecasts 10, 27–8, 40–2

Galveston, Texas 34
Guatemala 6, 24, 39
Gulf of Mexico 6, 10–11

Honduras 6, 24, 38–9
Hurricane Andrew 10–11, 34
Hurricane Camille 19, 33
Hurricane Fifi 24
Hurricane Hugo 8, 28
Hurricane Mitch 38–9
hurricane names 8–10
hurricane seasons 8
hurricane seedlings 17, 20,
    26–7, 40
hurricane sizes 5, 14–15, 18
hurricane speeds 27, 41
hurricane survival 28, 42
hurricane watch 28

Indian Ocean 6–7

Jamaica 6–7

Louisiana 6, 10–11

measuring hurricanes 22–3, 32
meteorologists 6, 9, 22–3, 40
Miami, Florida 6, 10–11
Mississippi 6, 19, 33
Mount Pinatubo 37
mudslides 37–9

National Hurricane Center,
    Florida, USA 23
Nicaragua 6, 38–9
northern hemisphere 8, 21

Pacific Ocean 6–7, 9, 15, 24,
    26–7
Philippines 6, 37

rain 4, 6, 14–15, 22, 24–5, 30,
    32–4, 36–9
research 41
rice paddies 13

Saffir, Herbert 23
Saffir-Simpson Scale 23
satellites 17, 26–7, 40
sewage 35
shelters 13, 35
Simpson, Robert 23
snakes 31
southern hemisphere 8, 21
storm surge 11, 13, 25, 29–31,
    33–4, 42
supplies 28–9, 39
thunderstorms 15, 17, 19, 21,
    26, 41
tornadoes 5, 19, 24
tropical storms 6–7, 17, 20–1,
    27, 37, 40
tropics 6, 14
typhoons 6–7, 9, 17, 26–7,
    36–7, 43

updraughts 17

volcanoes 37–8

warnings 11, 13, 28–9, 40, 42
water supplies 35
water temperature 14, 16,
    26–7, 36, 41
waves 4–5, 11–13, 18, 24–5,
    30–1
winds 4–7, 10–11, 13–14,
    18–24, 27, 30, 32–4, 36, 38,
    40, 43